ABOUT THE A

David Youell and Paula Downey have specialised in organisational communication since 1983, working at board and senior management level with national and international organisations to develop strategy and design practical communication solutions to workplace issues.

The principal partners at **downey youell associates**, a specialist communication practice based in Dublin Ireland, their wide experience and personal backgrounds embrace a number of key management functions and communication disciplines.

The Communication Dynamic — their unique personal development programme — is at the heart of their mission: to create a new awareness of the critical role communication plays in our living, working and being.

Exploring the

Communication Dynamic

301 Building Blocks to Enrich your Working Relationships

PAULA DOWNEY AND DAVID YOUELL

Oak Tree Press

Dublin

Oak Tree Press
Merrion Building, Lower Merrion Street
Dublin 2, Ireland
www.oaktreepress.com

© 1998 Paula Downey and David Youell

A catalogue record of this book is
available from the British Library.

ISBN 1 86076 109 7

All rights reserved. No part of this publication may be reproduced or transmitted in any form or by any means, including photocopying and recording, without written permission of the publisher. Such written permission must also be obtained before any part of this publication is stored in a retrieval system of any nature. Requests for permission should be directed to Oak Tree Press, Merrion Building, Lower Merrion Street, Dublin 2, Ireland.

Printed in the Republic of Ireland by Colour Books Ltd.

Exploring the
COMMUNICATION DYNAMIC

301 Building Blocks to Enrich your Working Relationships

One way or another, size matters! Measured in inches, this is a small book, but on each page you'll find an aspect of a topic so huge, it's arguably the biggest there is: human communication.

It's the downfall of organisations large and small . . . and the engine of the great enduring names. It's a common cause of business strife . . . yet the only real solution. It's at the heart of team and workplace hassles . . . and the sole creator of harmony and synergy. It's the great human separator . . . and yet it's the one thing that binds people together.

Not so much something we 'do' from time to time, communication is something we're *part of*, all of the time. It defines us, and colours our world. Whatever path we take in life, *communication is <u>the</u> core lifeskill*.

Take it apart and you soon realise that it can't be separated out from Life and Self, because communication is born in personal awareness and given expression through all of the activities we associate with human interaction and creation.

Communication is much more than words. It has to do with how we perceive and respond to the world, and the way we think. It's about our attitudes and behaviours and what they say about us. It's about honesty, integrity and credibility and the way our body speaks. And mostly, it's about *the other person,* so listening has a big part to play.

In organisations, communication is also about strategy and planning and measurement. It's about leadership and values, and *respect* for people and the community.

In writing this small book we had two things in mind: we wanted to create an accessible and practical guide for everyday use. And we wanted to begin to lift the lid off this complex and multi-faceted subject by presenting it in all its dimensions. We hope you will find it both instructional and inspirational.

Whether you open it for specific advice or dip into it at random, you'll find some of communication's essential truths to broaden your communication awareness. Nuggets of wisdom you can use in those critical moments when, by simply being more *conscious* of your role in this determining — and fragile — human process, you have an opportunity to make a real difference.

1

Communication is a commonplace word for a highly complex
activity, that affects everything we are and everything we do,
as individuals and organisations.

It is the currency of our human connectedness,
the architecture of every relationship, and the essence
of our living, working and being.

Communication defines us and our organisations,
colours our world, and creates our 'version' of reality.

2

Building trust is the process of articulating distrust.

When you openly express the fear, doubt or suspicion
that lies between you and others, the possibility
for developing 'trust' increases.

And trust is vital to effective communication.

3

Genuine listening requires the courage of an open mind.

4

Make new members of a team or regular group feel welcome by introducing them properly. Clarify why they're on board, who or what they represent, and what expertise or experience they bring to the table.

This is a vital communication task that group leaders often overlook.

5

In organisations, communication is the unseen hand that moulds the landscape in which the corporate strategy is played out.

It is the *single most important factor* in building a new reality. Or maintaining the status quo.

6

Relationships worth having, take time and effort.

(There are no short-cuts to anything worthwhile.)

7

Become familiar with the power of the pause in public speaking. It gives you time to gather your thoughts. It underlines what you're saying. And it's never as long as you think!

8

Whenever you ask, 'What do I need to communicate?' the answer is always '*Credibility*, first'.

Without that, you are lost.

9

Your opinion of someone, based on reputation alone, is not *your own.* When you 'know' someone by reputation, you know them second-hand — through someone else's eyes.

Borrowed opinion is no substitute for sound judgement based on personal observation, so clear your head and begin each interaction with a fresh page.

10

Every interaction is a relationship.
A pot pourri of individual contributions — physical, intellectual, emotional and spiritual. And each contribution matters.

With a partner of thirty years, or a local news vendor for thirty seconds, your contribution to the relationship can be good. Or bad. Or indifferent.

In every situation, you have a role.
And you have a choice.

11

True communication — creating understanding and sharing meaning — is about *content* and *process*. Not performance.

12

Before making that important telephone call, jot down the outcome you want, in a few words. Then list the main points you want to make and the questions you want to ask, and keep this in front of you during the call.

The three or four minutes you take to gather your thoughts could make all the difference.

13

The Concise Oxford Dictionary defines **Communicate** as:
'To succeed in conveying information or invoking understanding.'

(Note the word '*succeed*'.)

14

Treat the absence of conflict in any workgroup with healthy suspicion. It's almost always phoney.

Disagreement is a natural consequence of different personalities and points of view converging. It's *un*natural to suppress it.

When you skirt around the tension and pretend that all is well, the pressure just goes underground until another time.
It doesn't go away.

Conflict is normal, healthy, and potentially creative.

15

When two people meet, two different sets of 'software' are talking to each other.

Hooking up successfully requires a workable interface between the 'software' platforms.

16

The best speeches are supported by *passion* and *depth of knowledge* — not slides and audio-visual aids.

17

THIS WAY UP!

Remember, information doesn't always arrive
in the condition it was sent.

18

Our life experiences sculpt the mental maps
by which we negotiate the world.

Everyone's map is different. Everyone 'sees' things differently,
thinks differently and as a result *behaves* differently.

And differences cause friction.

Instead of striving for 'sameness' try to appreciate and value
different points of view and search for practical ways to use
the differences productively.

19

The truth is simple, if sometimes painful.

Practice speaking the truth *pleasantly* —
and avoid settling for the anaesthetic of pleasant *un*truth.

20

Close friendships thrive on disclosure.

Nothing erodes intimacy like withholding, so if you're faced with a communication 'chasm', consider if all the cards are on the table. On both sides.

21

Are you a contributor to the junk mail nightmare?

❐ GUILTY   ❐ NOT GUILTY

Consider how many form letters you routinely junk.
Now ask: 'Why should anyone read *mine*?'

> Be environmentally conscious.
> Be people conscious.
> Write *purposeful* letters.

22

Stories are potent communicators. A good story will be remembered long after the 'ten-step-strategy' (or whatever you're pitching) has been forgotten.

Is there a parable, fairy-tale, myth, or some wonderful metaphor or real-life comparison that captures the essence of your theme or central idea?

23

No one has to listen.

It is the communicator's challenge to command attention.

24

'Economy Size' means 'small' in motor cars
but 'extra large' in washing powder.

Aristotle was keen on definition. He insisted that every word
should indicate one thing only — and where there was a possibility
of confusion, the exact intended meaning should be defined
before any further deductive reasoning could take place.

'Definition' is as important today as it was in 350 BC.

25

Disagreement is the child of two different
and perfectly valid views of the world.

There is no right. And no wrong.
Just different ways of seeing.

26

After you've inserted the last full stop in that report, weed out unnecessary, superfluous, nonessential, clichéd, old-fashioned, irrelevant words that clutter, camouflage or otherwise disguise your central point.

Find alternatives to dry business-speak: *'I refer to yours of...'* vs *'Thanks for your letter'*. Ditch passive expressions for active verbs: *'Recruitment policies were updated'* vs *'We updated recruitment policies'*. Drop *'aforementioned'*, *'above'*, *'below'*, *'heretofore'* and any other dead weight you can find.

And the surviving words will matter more.

27

If you want people to be committed to your idea, your project, your plan or your organisation, look for ways to involve them.

No one will put significant weight behind something they don't feel part of.

28

Take notes at meetings. Constantly.
It keeps your mind focused on what's being said *right now*.

(You'll also have a useful log of what took place.)

29

You don't have to be chat-show host material
to engage an audience.

Captivating presenters give generously of *themselves*.
Beyond technique, they've mastered the art of caring more for
the value the audience receives than for their own performance.

30

The words you choose (including those you choose to avoid) reveal your underlying attitudes and values.

31

Intuition allows shafts of insight to penetrate
habitual ways of thinking.

But in the western world the 'rational' muscle
is over-exercised at the expense of intuition.

A deeper faith in the intuitive side of your nature
will sharpen your observation of events around you,
and enhance your response to others.

32

Always look beyond behavioural blackspots.

Deep down, we all want to be loved
and appreciated.

You. Me. And the person who just made you angry.

33

W̲ith an 's' or without an 's'?

Communications — with an 's' — usually refers to communication *technology* — phones, faxes, e-mail and so on. It can also refer to trains and boats and planes.

For clarity, use communication without an 's' when you mean the sharing of meaning or the generation of understanding.

34

Be on time for meetings.

Turning up late communicates a strong signal to others: you value your time more than theirs.

35

Don't stand in front of the projector.

(Incredible, but true. People *do* this — all the time! And a presenter with this month's sales figures or a map of North America on their face is more distracting than convincing.)

36

Would people recognise you from the way you write?

Apply the 'Would-I-say-this-to-a-friend?' test when writing a letter, and change any expression you wouldn't normally use in conversation with someone you know.

One of the principles of successful communication is to treat the other person as a friend. Write the way you speak, and see the difference it makes.

37

The body speaks first — and usually louder.

Overemphasis on delivery and not enough time spent preparing or evaluating, is frequently the reason why communication initiatives in business miss the mark.

The *'30-20-50'* Good Practice Rule of thumb:

> Prepare 30%
> Deliver 20%
> Evaluate 50%

39

Develop a philosophy of service towards others.

When you attend to their needs fully and willingly,
you communicate respect and cultivate trust.

We are *all* in the service business.
(What other human industry is there?)

40

Small gestures send big smoke signals,
especially when they concern core values.

Leaders: Look around. Are your practices, rules and rituals
consistent with your words? Or is there a credibility gap?

(For example: Consider how many companies talk a storm on
'equality' yet retain executive car park spaces and separate
canteens. Ooops sorry — executive *dining rooms*!)

41

Don't ask one message to serve more than one purpose.

42

Next time you hear someone say *'I made it perfectly clear...'*
ask the simple question: How do you know?

Because understanding happens in the mind of the other person, it doesn't matter how crisp and clear you think your transmission may have been — reception is never guaranteed.

If you want to make it perfectly clear, don't just say it.
Say it, and *check* for understanding.

43

LISTEN!

At least 50% of the communication process
is about what you hear, not what you say.

Don't be a motor-mouth!

44

The telephone has limitations.

It's okay for sending words, but as a communication device it falls short because so much of what we say, we say *without* words.

So if the conversation's an important one, make it face-to-face.

45

The quality of a company's communication
is a reflection of its culture.

This is either good news, or bad news!

46

Everyone has an invisible 'bubble' of personal space around them. There are different zones from distant to intimate, and access by 'outsiders' is by invitation only and strictly on the basis of the relationship at the time.

Respect for each other's 'bubble' is usually instinctive, but sometimes signals can be misread and you can find yourself in the wrong zone!

Trespassers will usually find communication difficult. Even impossible.

47

Create positive mirrors.

Send out good feelings,
and see how they are reflected back
by those around you.

48

Take a risk and step out from behind the lectern. Physically join the audience or group and turn 'me and you' into 'we and us'.

(People have come to see *you*, not listen to a talking box.)

49

You can't 'give' meaning to someone. Meaning springs from the
other person's internal process of interpreting, reflecting on,
and evaluating data.

You can present *data*, but the same data can mean
different things to different people, so meaning is very personal.

When you succeed in sharing the *same* meaning,
you've managed to communicate.

50

How is it that poor communication is
always someone else's fault?

51

Closed questions clarify. They're the ones that elicit a one-word response: *Yes. No. Tuesday. Twenty-five. New York. Midnight...*

Closed questions are conversation cul-de-sacs.

Use *How did you...?* instead of *Did you...?* And *What is your view...?* in place of *Do you agree...?* And don't forget *Why?* and *Tell me about...* and *How do you feel about...?*

Open questions oil the wheels of conversation.

52

Trust is like honesty, or pregnancy. You can't be a little bit pregnant, or a little bit honest, or a little bit trustworthy. Or trustworthy when it suits you.

Trust is a long term, permanent position.

53

Research your audience and pitch your message at the right level. Get it wrong and you'll either patronise them by oversimplifying, or shoot clear over their heads.

Either way, you've lost them.

54

Personal awareness is the badge of the master communicator.
How can you understand feelings in others if you
don't recognise and understand your own?

Start to understand others
by getting to know the person in your bathroom mirror.

55

Good communicators remember people's names.

You can improve your skill by using the other person's name
in your conversation as soon as possible
after you've been introduced.

56

Why use two words if one will do?

57

With more than 200 non-verbal signals to choose from (more than any other creature) humans are capable of highly subtle communication — without the need for words.

58

Inject power into your requests for help by stating *clearly* what you want, and say how it will help you.

People are more willing to help when they understand how their input will make a difference.

59

Different viewpoints can lead to friction, especially when you're hell-bent on defending your position. But watch how conflict starts to crumble when you focus on the 'opposition' — and try to understand them.

Understanding is the arch-enemy of conflict.

Because more than anything else — *more than being right* — human beings need to feel *understood*.

60

Arrive in time to check out the a-v.

There's nothing quite like a blank TV screen, an out-of-focus OHP or upside-down-and-back-to-front slides to get fingers tapping and attention slipping.

(By the way, there is nothing original or witty that hasn't been said about technology on the blink. So save your breath!)

61

Technology makes communication faster, not *necessarily* better.

62

In the first few minutes of meeting someone,
as much as 95% of what's going on is non-verbal.

(So much for the pithy opening remark!
That's a tiny part of the exchange.)

63

The important things in life are the things we *give*,
not the things we take.

In communication too, practice giving to the other person,
and you'll get what you need.

Giving *is* receiving.

64

A 'presentation' doesn't have to happen on a platform before a captive audience. You're presenting your case whenever you have to *persuade*.

Before you engage, consider:
Should this be a presentation? Or just a conversation?

65

'Thank you for a really enjoyable dinner'.
'Thank you for the order'.
'Thank you for your help'.
'Thank you for being a friend'.

'Thank you' is one of the shortest
yet most important letters you can write.

66

Anger is a barrier to communication. It 'screens out' intelligence and makes it harder to hear and harder to be heard.

To be respected and believed, communication must be regular and timely. Not after the event. Not when there's a spare moment. Not when you happen to remember it.

Regular and timely means: *regular* and *timely*.

68

The English language has about a million words to choose from. Yet most of us choose from about three thousand or less.

Next time you hear or read a new word, look it up and use it. The more ways you have to describe what you think or feel, the closer you'll get to saying what you really mean.

(Do crosswords to grow your vocabulary.)

69

Cultivate personal wisdom.
It's the only communication compass you need.

70

We can too easily pooh-pooh those who aren't like-minded.
The truth is, we need each other.

Left-brainers benefit from a sprinkling of Right-brain imagination.
And Right-brainers sometimes need a dash of logic from the Left.

A little judicious seasoning is the secret ingredient
of most successful teams, because *whole*-brain thinking
produces the best ideas.

71

You may be on top of your topic, but if you're uptight and wobbly, you'll fail the credibility test.

Relax, and focus on tone.

72

When you call someone on their cellphone, ask if it's convenient for them to talk *before* launching in to what you want to say.

If you *receive* a call when you're with someone, ask if it's okay for you to take it.

Show consideration for others.

73

So-called 'power-dressing' is just another (not very subtle) way of attempting to establish dominance over others.

And dominance, whatever package it arrives in, is a barrier, not a gateway, to communication.

74

Good communicators intuitively switch between three 'positions':

1. Where I'm at (*Concerned with <u>my</u> wants and needs*)
2. Where you're at (*Concerned with <u>your</u> wants and needs*)
3. Detached observation (*Stepping back to take an impartial view of what's happening*)

Be conscious of the danger of getting stuck in any one position and psychologically switch from time to time to keep communication flowing.

(Two people stuck in 'Where I'm at' are going nowhere!)

75

Often, the most eloquent and compelling communication is silence. Knowing when *not* to speak, when *not* to respond to a letter, or when to simply hold your tongue, can be more powerful than words.

76

Enthusiasm is catching.
In its presence, and in its absence.

77

Communication technology is supposed to make life easier. When it feels like it's controlling *you*, it's time to take some drastic action.

Stop feeding the system! Why not leave your cellphone at home today? Or decide you're *not* going to check your e-mail messages for a day or two?

You'll live!

78

You have two ears and one mouth. Use them proportionately.

(An oldie, but a goodie.)

Pay close attention to opposing points of view. Each one is an opportunity to improve your understanding of the truth about your world and the people who inhabit it.

As you come to appreciate the structures and pressures within which *everyone* lives their lives, your empathy and compassion for others will blossom.

80

Only use zippy slogans and positive 'success' posters *after* you've done the groundwork in the hearts-and-minds department.

Slogans and posters reinforce messages.
They don't change attitudes.

81

When positions and opinions are locked-in,
the potential to communicate is locked out.

Lack of tolerance of another's position is truly
one of the greatest barriers to co-operation between people.

82

Perception *is* reality.

83

Studies show we put greater faith in the *emotional* information we get from *non-verbal* signals than the *factual* information we get from *verbal* ones.

Which means there's a real possibility of recruiting someone or deciding to do business with them because you happen to like them — even when the evidence suggests otherwise.

84

*F*orce, fight, block, takeover, dominate, dictate, beat, wipe-out, confront, shake-up, drive-up, push, thrust, tackle, attack, defeat, cut-and-thrust, fear, loss, worst-case scenario, nightmare situation, on the offensive, suffer, survival, power base, aggressive, hostile...

The harsh language of business.
Is it any wonder it feels like a battle?

85

On the telephone your voice is all you've got.
Don't make that call if you are angry. Or nervous. (Or drunk.)

86

When you've reached the end of your rope with someone, and your patience is about to break, take a deep breath and make one more attempt to get through.

Give patience one last chance.

87

Your presentation should be a collective experience, not a one-man show, so involve your audience.

Paint word pictures. Pose challenging questions. Ask them to recall a relevant personal experience. *Get their brains in gear!*

88

Don't shift the blame.

If you are not being understood, that's *your* problem.

89

On your voicemail or ansaphone, respect callers' time by keeping your outgoing message short.

And keep the messages you leave for others brief and to the point. Clearly state the reason for your call, and always add the date and time.

90

'People skill' is the ability to identify and respond appropriately to the moods, motives and needs of others.

91

Well thought-out headings and sub-headings make it easier for the reader to navigate your document.

92

When conflict comes your way, shoulder your share of the responsibility. It mightn't be possible to change the other person, but it *is* possible to change two fundamentals:
your attitude, and *your* response.

When *you* change, the equation changes.

93

We remember just 5% of what we hear, 25% of what we see, but about 90% of what we do.

So if you want people to really grasp your ideas, don't just *tell* them. Find ways for them to *see* and *experience* what you mean.

94

Recognise that everyone sees the world, not as it is, but as *they are*, and compensate accordingly.

(People make judgements on the basis of *their* attitudes and values, not yours.)

95

Don't underestimate the power of authenticity.

(In an age of hype and subterfuge it's a scarce commodity, and its glow can be detected miles away.)

96

If you happen to be 'vertically advantaged', remember that tall people can intimidate short people — without uttering a single word.

So, find a way to narrow the gap if you can.
Both sitting usually helps.

(The best dialogue happens when both parties are on the level, in every sense of the word.)

97

Communication is not about delivering messages, it's about sharing meaning.

(Delivering messages is for motorcycle couriers.)

98

Quieten your inner voice.

If you're mentally rehearsing an Oscar-winning response, you're not listening. And if you're not listening, how can you respond appropriately?

Only when you stop practising your own script is it possible to truly listen.

99

Men and women *do* have different qualities — but generalising on the basis of gender is a dangerous game.

Not *all* women think or behave the same. Not all men do either.

100

In industry, 'adding value' means doing something to raw material to make it worth more than it was worth as raw material.

Words are the raw material of verbal communication.
Choose them wisely to give your message added value.

101

Find a way to get personal agendas, motives and needs out in the open.

There's always an agenda, even between two people, and that's okay. But 'agendas in the air' can fuel silent mistrust and cause communication shutdown, breakdown — even meltdown!

102

Have an 'Show-and-Tell Day' once a year, when every team presents their work in a fun way to colleagues.

(When you know what other people do, and how they contribute to the bigger picture, it's hard to maintain the Us-and-Them barricades that hinder relationships.)

Proximity can blur objectivity.

If you feel too close to your topic don't be afraid to seek out an interested and informed second opinion about what you want to say and how you should to say it.

104

When we share our failures, we celebrate hard-earned wisdom —
and we all learn. But it's risky. Sharing is about openness and truth
and where the illusion of perfection is the norm,
it's hard to admit weakness.

Somewhere along the way, openness and truth become optional
as we discover that to survive and fly high, we must keep
part of ourselves tucked away and hidden.

But is that survival? Or just a slower death?

105

A well-placed word of praise, a generous pat on the back, can travel a long way.

You may never know how far. You may even discover that what goes around, comes around. To you.

106

Manage group feedback by listing each point raised before you respond to any of them.

By taking the temperature of the meeting in this way you can include everyone's point of view, and make sure the discussion doesn't get bogged down by one person, or one issue.

107

If you lack confidence about speaking in public, start to *act as if* you have complete confidence.

Think of yourself as a confident communicator and one day you'll wake up to discover — you *are*!

108

'Oh, don't be so emotional!'

In the name of all that's *human*,
what's wrong with being emotional?

Feelings and emotions are at the very core of the
human condition and affect the way we communicate
at the most fundamental level. Suppressing them — or
expecting them to be suppressed — is *un*natural.

Our feelings and emotions make us uniquely human.
Give them wings.

How many e-mails greeted you this morning?
How many were necessary?

It's an epidemic! Innocent civilians are drowning —
in other people's thoughtless litter.

Be a self-appointed litter warden. Put the onus on the sender
to observe a simple protocol, that every message opens with a
one line introduction: 'This is important to you because…'

And as a sender, apply the same Relevance Test.
People have enough on their plate without you adding to the pile.

Corporate Communication Health Check

On a scale of 1 to 10 how does your organisation rate?

a. People here are authentic, not superficial
b. Different points of view are respected
c. Time spent communicating is regarded as an investment, not a cost
d. We aren't afraid to speak honestly — even about the tough stuff
e. We're encouraged to question, argue, and challenge the status quo
f. We have the skills we need to communicate in this way.

Personal Communication Health Check

On a scale of 1 to 10, how do *you* rate?

a. I always speak in an open and direct way
b. I see every person as unique and valuable
c. I'm conscious that friction is the result of different thinking
d. I spend more time trying to understand other perspectives than promoting my own
e. I try to 'get inside' other people's heads by asking questions about their beliefs
f. I'm not afraid to change my point of view after listening to someone else.

112

Let's ban 'but'.

'But' is like an eraser. It has the effect of cancelling out what's gone before. (*'I hear what you're saying, but...'*)

Use 'and' or 'although' instead of 'but', to open up your mind and *build* on what's gone before.

113

Winston Churchill, Mahatma Gandhi, John F Kennedy, Martin Luther King, Nelson Mandela....

Great leadership and great communication go hand in hand.

Genuine communication is based in truth.

Attempts to 'sell smoke' have a habit of choking the sender as well as the receiver. Sooner or later.

115

Only 10% of your communication is carried by the words you use. Your voice, the *way* you use it and your body language, account for a whacking 90% of the total message you transmit.

If you doubt the power of non-verbal signals, consider how a conversation can be blown off course by a sideways look or a knowing smile.

116

Create visual images that bring technical
or dry academic information to life.

It's easier to imagine something 'as tall as two houses'
than 'eighteen metres long' (unless you're addressing a group of
slide-rule-carrying, number-crunching structural engineers!)

The more *appropriate* the image is to the audience,
the stronger the impact.

117

When you're in the wrong, apologise without hesitation, unconditionally, and straight from the heart.

118

Ring-ring. Ring-ring. Ring-ring....
'ALL OPERATORS ARE BUSY. PLEASE HOLD.'

♪.... *OOOOOOOOHH-KLAHOMA, where-the-sun-shines-brightly-on-the-plains...* ♪♪ 'PLEASE HOLD.' ♪....*There's NO business like SHOW business like NO business I know - da-da-da-da-da-da-da-da-daa-daaaaa....* ♪♪ 'PLEASE HOLD' ♪... *gonna wash that man right outta my hair, I'm gonna wash...* ♪♪ 'GOOD MORNING, CAN I HELP YOU?'

Pass me my dancing shoes!!

Alternatively, listen to your music-on-hold and see if it's adding to your corporate identity. Or interfering with it.

119

Dishonesty has no long-term future.

If you want to improve participation in a group where the regular team leader is the assured, outgoing, 'driven'-type, get someone else to chair the meeting once in a while.

Team spirit can rise dramatically when the leader is subject to the same rules as everyone else. (And their listening skills often improve miraculously!)

Democracy works, at work.

121

Don't reduce people to simplistic labels.

Capitalist, Sexist, Feminist, Racist... Labels are interpersonal shortcuts, but human beings are complex individuals and stereotyping can be seriously wide of the mark.

Identify a favourite stereotype — and drop it.

122

When a relationship flounders, walking the other way may distance you from the problem. But it won't make it disappear.

If you value the relationship, don't let the bad stuff pile up. Address the matter in an appropriate and *timely* way — before it has time to grow too big, or too hot to handle.

(The stuff you push under the carpet will inevitably trip you up.)

123

Communication is not something you do.
It's something you're *part of*.

124

Avoid slang, jargon, gobbledegook and the other unwritten group conventions that build an invisible wall around you and your inner circle. They can become subtle ways of excluding others and generating negative feelings.

Be awake to group code which may unwittingly communicate *'Go away!'* to others.

125

'To whom it may concern'

A name is very personal. And people are often quite sensitive about it. They like to hear it used, they like to see it in print, and they *hate* to see it misspelt.

If you want to kill your communication stone dead, start your letter with *'Dear Sir/Madam'*. Or use the wrong name. Or the incorrect spelling.

Any of these options should do the trick.

What managers want to tell new hires is not always
what new hires want to know. Not yet.

Each is at a different place.

Management sees the bigger picture: The Vision and the Mission, the Strategy and Results. While new employee focus is on 'me' and 'my (smaller) world': pay, conditions, the canteen food and how I join the sports club — what HR people tag 'Comp & Bens'.

Communication with new people has to start from where *they* are, and move outwards to the wider scene.
Not from where you are, and move in.

With induction as in all things, human nature rules ok. Answer basic needs before expecting people to consider higher things.

127

Smile on the telephone, especially when you say hello and when you end the call. The other person may not be able to see it, but they will certainly sense it.

128

People don't change their minds because you want them to. They change because *they* want to. Because *their* needs will be met.

If you need to persuade someone, don't try to talk them into submission. Get off your soapbox. Establish their needs first. Then find a way to serve both.

Get to know your paradigms: the assumptions and prejudices you unwittingly use to limit yourself — and everyone around you.

When you get past limiting preconceptions, you open up a world of possibilities with those you meet along the Path of Life.

130

Jumping to conclusions
can be a dangerous way to exercise the mind.

131

If you're going to read your speech
you might as well mail it to your audience.

Learn to speak without notes. Invest in a book on memory technique or find out how actors remember their lines, and let your thoughts come from your heart.

People never listen to instructions as well as you expect them to. Don't assume understanding. Check for it.

And when you're on the receiving end, repeat complex instructions. *'Do you mean that...'* or *'So what you're saying is...'* will take just a minute — but might save you valuable hours.

133

You can do much to calm 'speaker's nerves' by identifying where the tension is coming from. Is the fear logical? Psychological? Or emotional?

Some fears *are* justified, but often they're just feelings in the heart. Inventions of the mind.

When you can pinpoint the source and see it for what it is, you feel more in control, and the 'butterflies' subside.

134

The silent signals your body transmits can strengthen or weaken your words, reinforce or undermine your meaning, reflect or betray your mood.

Remember it's the whole body that communicates — not just the voice — so what you think you're saying may not be what your listener hears.

135

Conflict is an opportunity to revise perspectives, improve understanding and deepen relationships.

Only by working *through* conflict do we mature and grow, intellectually, emotionally and spiritually.

No pain. No gain.

136

The way your document looks
says as much about *you* as your words.

The medium should add to your message,
not take away from it, or overshadow it.
Plenty of 'air' on the page is easier on the eye
than text crammed edge to edge.

Don't be stingy with space.

137

People believe that if they can talk or write they can communicate.

It ain't necessarily so.

The communication dynamic is the heart of the matter.
It's the essence of our living, working and being.

The more we are aware of it, in all its dimensions, and the more we understand its influence and its power to *transform* our lives, the greater our contribution can be.

Whatever road we travel.

139

When you're listening, concentrate as if you'll have to pass on what you hear to someone else. When you change your attitude to the information — from listener to teacher — you'll hear and understand much more.

140

Condense your core message into one memorable sentence your audience can take away with them, and repeat it several times throughout your presentation — especially at the end.

141

When someone keeps asking the same question,
don't assume they haven't heard the answer.

It could be *they* don't feel heard.
Or understood.

Organisations are the 'media' of business.

Through the products and services they *choose* to provide, the working environment they *choose* to create, the behaviours they *choose* to reward — or punish — they sponsor and communicate the values that ultimately define our world.

What is your organisation transmitting to the world?

143

Don't let your conversation become a one-way street!
Talking *at* people or engaging in non-stop monologue
is *transmission*, not communication. And it's boring.

Nobody likes wall-to-wall talk.
And no-one loses listeners faster than a bore.

(Besides, over-talkers never learn from other people.)

144

Master the art of the Executive Summary.

So-called 'executives' are not the only people too busy/lazy/disinterested to plough through the whole report. Not everyone *needs* to.

Sum up your argument or proposal in a succinct opening that hammers home your central theme. You'll satisfy those who don't need wads of detail. And you'll hook those who do.

145

Be completely open to the fact that you may be completely wrong. Especially when you're convinced that you're completely right.

Don't be a 'flat-earther'.

146

The censor in you is seldom off-duty. Motivated largely by fear — fear of rejection, fear of punishment, fear of failure, fear of being wrong — we all hold back or hide things about ourselves.

Withholding is not necessarily a bad thing, but often we self-censor something that *should* be said, because we lack the courage to be open.

When you consciously share your thoughts and feelings in an open and appropriate way, you build trust, encourage empathy and deepen understanding.

147

If you knew this conversation, letter, e-mail or telephone call was your last — would you do it differently?

How would you like to be remembered?

148

It takes two.

And if one person doesn't respond, it's like throwing the ball at an open window instead of a closed door.

When there's no response, it's amazing how quickly steam goes out of an argument.

149

It's a business truism: What gets measured gets done.
What doesn't, becomes optional.

The days when communication could be left to chance
are well and truly over. If you're not measuring your impact,
you're flying blind.

150

CREDIBILITY WARNING!

Make sure your overhead slides are in order *before* you start your presentation!

151

Interpersonal communication happens within a context.
Organisational communication is interpersonal communication
in a *business* context.

Managing comunication is the subtle and ongoing process
of managing the physical, social and psychological *context*
in which relationships happen in the workplace.

Context is king! Because it's the *context*
that gives meaning to meaning.

152

The eyes are the windows to the soul. That's where you'll find real clues to what others are thinking and feeling.

(Why do you think lovers stare into each other's eyes so intently?)

153

If you're invited to be one of a panel of speakers, insist on knowing what the others are speaking about to avoid overlap.

The sweat and soaring blood pressure you feel when your carefully prepared points are delivered by the speaker before you, isn't worth it. And the audience won't appreciate the re-run.

The heart, lungs, liver, kidneys and the brain, are like different 'departments' of the body. Each with its own job to do, but totally dependent on all the others.

Any disruption to the vital blood supply between departments has serious implications for the health of the entire system.

Communication is the lifeblood of organisations.

155

Culture is fundamentally shaped by
the attitudes and behaviour of leaders.

They're the human bulletin boards
advertising the values that are rewarded.

Walk talks.

Understanding oils the wheels of change.

Employees need to understand the bigger picture before they can be expected to hitch their wagon to your vision of a new tomorrow.

People don't fear change. They fear *being* changed.
And uncertainty.

157

Two rules to add real value to the spoken or the written word: Start strong. And end strong.

158

Meetings are time-consuming and expensive,
so make sure yours are productive.

When calling a meeting be clear about the purpose and
the kind of participation you expect. Leave enough time
for contributions. And summarise the outcome and decisions
reached at the end, so everyone knows what has been achieved.

(How often do you leave a meeting wondering
'What on earth was that all about?')

159

If you're interested in human behaviour, study the Myers-Briggs
matrix of personality types and the different ways
people approach the world.

It's easier to deal with others
when you can see where they're coming from.

160

Purposeful communication is strategy in action.

It emerges from the business strategy and supports
the organisation all the way towards its objectives.

It responds to real needs, and produces measurable results.

161

Words matter. They shape your thoughts.
And your thoughts shape the attitudes and behaviour
that make you what you are.

Words like *agree, care, independent, good, sincere, heart, love, special, hope,* are warm and positive. Words like *afraid, doubt, risk, abnormal, can't, disagree, dislike, unfair, unfortunately,* are cold and negative.

Words change the way we feel about things.

162

Tests have shown that immediately after listening to a ten-minute presentation, the average listener has *heard, understood, evaluated, and remembered* about *half* of what was said. Within 48 hours, that drops by about another 50%!

A scary thought, considering how much time we spend in 'listening mode'.

163

Communication is always worth the thinking time. The more *thought-through* a project's communication strategy, the more vigorous and successful it will be.

164

If your conversation is in a tailspin, a psychological gear change from negative to positive will drive the interaction on to firmer ground.

165

Skilled communicators read body language as easily as text.

166

It's easy to be seduced by the latest technology. But technology makes no difference to the quality of *communication*.

Communication is the story, not the word processor.
The painting, not the palette.
The compliment, not the pen.

Technology is not communication. It's the *enabler*.

167

Experts often have a hard time opening up to concepts and ideas outside the familiar boundaries of their own patch.

No one — not even you — has all the answers, so beware of being closed to new ideas.

History's awash with 'experts' who got it wrong.

168

Never fear your audience. They *want* you to do well.

If things do go wrong they'll be rooting for you to get back on track, so don't get stuck in silent self-recrimination. Smooth over the crack with a little bit of humour (if you can manage it) or a little bit of honesty (if you can't).

And move swiftly along.

169

Talk is cheap. Talk is aspirational.
No amount of *talk* will get the bus to its destination.
Someone has to get into the cab and drive it there.

Sooner or later, every Grand Plan deteriorates
into somebody having to *do* something!

An organisation's reputation or public image is the sum total of everyone's experience of the organisation.

Those who work in it and their families. Customers and clients, suppliers and shareholders, members and neighbours. Even competitors. Everyone who experiences the organisation, its product or service, either directly or indirectly.

That's why every interaction, every *relationship*, is critical. Each one another brick in the wall. Another brushstroke on the canvas.

171

The perfect marriage of minds
Respects what has gone before,
And cherishes what is to come.

Considers, not what separate pasts
You glory in, but what future
You represent together.

(You can't vision the future, if you're anchored in the past.)

172

Always be clear.

If you can, say 'Yes' and mean it. Or 'No' and mean it.
Or explain clearly why you cannot make a decision.

People prefer decisiveness to shilly-shallying.

Answer three questions when planning your content:

1. *Who am I talking to?* (Who is the audience? Listener, reader, viewer...)
2. *How can I reach them?* (What is the best medium?)
3. *What response do I want?* (What do I want to happen?)

Then, and only then, should you ask: *What do I want to say?*

174

Thinking differently is a prelude to change.

Rediscover the personal touch:

Institute a 'Let's Talk' campaign by nominating a day each week when e-mail and voice mail are off-limits between people who sit within bickering distance of each other.

176

'How are you?' can be an empty habit or a genuine question.

When you ask: *'How are you?'*
listen to the answer.

(If you don't care, why ask?)

Think about it. Anything you ever achieved, you first achieved in your mind. You *saw* the goal. The new house. The foreign holiday. The change of career...

Organisations need a vision too, and it's no use locked up in the executive suite. It has to be *championed* by everyone.

Sharing the vision is the most important communication challenge facing any leader, in organisations of any size.

178

Advertising copywriters work hard to pack
maximum power into minimum words.

'Beanz Meanz Heinz', *'Guinness Is Good For You'*,
'Butter is the Cream' and other well known catch-phrases
work well because they carry meaning beyond the words.

Can your message be captured in a
succinct and memorable phrase?

179

Physiognomy is a powerful communicator.

Hunched up shoulders and a worried frown.
Head held high and a broad smile.
Each tells a different story.

A positive physiognomy looks good.
And it feels good!

In the emerging business paradigm, people are at the centre. So *in*tangibles like trust, openness, co-operation, flexibility, service are high-value items on the corporate shopping list.

None of these things are available off-the-shelf.
They have to be cultivated and nourished. And that puts communication right at the heart of tomorrow's company.

181

If you make the call, it's up to you to end it.

If you're one of the people who find this hard to do, decide beforehand what you want from the conversation and end it politely and efficiently when you've achieved what you set out to do.

Slides that capture a complex idea or concept in a word or memorable visual, can add real value to your presentation. But those that look like wiring diagrams hinder, rather than help communication.

(Unless of course they're *meant* to be wiring diagrams!)

Keep two words in mind when designing slides:
Synthesise and *Simplify*.

183

Criticising people in their absence
says more about the criticiser than the criticised.

Don't be a behind-the-hand critic.

184

If you think appearance is superficial, you're mistaken.
Looks reach down to our primal core and lead us to make instant,
sometimes totally unfounded positive *or* negative assumptions
about people.

Attraction and aversion are very personal. They're always about
you — not the other person. And they are usually linked to the
past, and not the present moment.

We are drawn to some and turned off by others. But be careful
you're not unconsciously screening people in *or* out,
merely on the basis of how they look.

There's more to a book than its cover.

185

They say: Actions speak louder than words.

Whoever *they* are, they're right.

186

Don't launch that communication initiative based on assumptions about the audience. Do the necessary work to turn the assumptions into facts, and target your communication finely.

The 'scatter-gun' approach is less effective, wasteful of resources, and can leave you with more problems than you started out with.

187

On the telephone your sweet voice travels *directly* into the other person's ear, so it's nice not to be doing anything else with your mouth at the time.

Chewing gum, eating, slurping coffee and smoking are among the worst offenders.

If you wouldn't do it in person, don't do it on the phone.

188

Never ask staff for feedback
unless you intend to act on what you learn.

189

A 'fair and just' decision is fair and just for *all* concerned.
And often this requires a laying down of personal wants
and needs, in favour of the higher purpose.

When this happens openly and honestly, attitudes and behaviour
change and even words and language take on more conciliatory
tone. And the outcome changes for the better.

The higher purpose is always greater
than the individual difference.

190

We express emotions and establish relationships almost *exclusively* through non-verbal communication.

191

Watch your language!

If you talk 're-engineering' and 'restructuring'
and refer to your business as a 'well-oiled machine'
don't be surprised if the people who work there feel more like
machine parts, than human beings — with feelings.

192

You're entitled to your point of view.
But you're not entitled to force-feed it to anyone else.

Communication is not about colonising people's minds.
It's about finding common ground.

A place where minds can meet.

193

Successful advertisements speak to both sides of the brain: they *appeal* to the emotional Right, and *convince* the logical Left.

Being attracted to an idea and being convinced or persuaded enough to take action are two different responses.

Powerful messages that deliver,
are both attractive *and* convincing.

194

Falling in love requires no words.
Falling *out* of love requires little else.

That's because falling *in love* is 'other-person' centred,
while falling *out of* love is self-centred.

The best communication is 'other-person' centred.

195

Every employee is a roving ambassador.

If the internal reality doesn't match the external 'promise',
you can depend on your people to spread it around.
Inconsistency is a time bomb waiting to explode —
usually when you can least afford trouble.

Is it time to dust down your employee communication strategy
and consider your ambassadors' credentials?

196

If you deliver your presentation in the same monotone, at the same speed, or rooted to the spot, don't be surprised if your audience drifts — or nods off.

Speed it up. Slow it down. Vary your rhythm and pace. And move around where you can.

Add some fizz!

197

Truth beats at the heart of good relationships.

Being true to yourself and truthful to others
is the path to genuine communication.

198

Human beings use all sorts of physical tricks
to establish dominance.

Taking up more space by standing to full height,
feet apart, hands on hips and elbows sticking out.
Pointing and touching. Staring more, smiling less.
Speaking louder. Talking and interrupting more.

Truly great people don't need tricks.
Their presence and influence is in their *being*.

199

Nurture an open mind.

Remember, no one has the complete picture of reality.

Including you.

(If we all had the complete picture, we'd all be in agreement all the time, and the world would be a quiet and rather boring place!)

200

Don't assume people know where you are coming from.

Like an athlete going for the jump, help your listener to understand
the context of what you're saying by taking a few steps back
to lead them into the subject.

Don't go back *too* far, however, before sprinting forward —
or you may find the spectators have abandoned the track!

Communication difficulties don't appear overnight.
They take time to develop. And they need time to be resolved.

('Quick-fix' solutions have an irritating habit
of unravelling very quickly.)

202

There are no new ideas.
Just timeless wisdom emerging in contemporary form.

Read the classic philosophers and scholars, and don't be afraid to
quote them if they've articulated your thoughts and feelings.
The words you find compelling may also strike a chord in others.

203

Conflict tests communication competence.

204

Reviewing the past and rehearsing the future while engaged in the present is the enemy of successful communication.

Learn to observe with a quiet mind. You'll see what's happening more accurately and respond more appropriately. And you'll never again want to bite your lip because of an unguarded or unhelpful remark.

Follow the simple instruction: *Be still. Be fully present.*

205

When the news is bad, Truth is your most powerful ally.

206

Our sense of territory is primal.

Like animals, we claim, mark, and defend our patch. And just as animals do, we feel safer and more confident on home ground.

When your personal confidence is on the line or under threat, try to locate the exchange on *your* territory.

207

Checklist for successful meetings:

Make sure
- The purpose is clear to everyone
- The participants understand their role
- The chairperson is on top of the topic
- There's enough time to get through the agenda
- The location is suitable (Not too hot, cold, big, small, noisy)

208

Like an iceberg, most of the true self is hidden.
So you seldom know people as well as you think.

Only by diving beneath your own surface
can you deepen your insight into others.

You are the laboratory.
In the immortal words: Know Thyself!

209

It takes longer to write a short and concise letter than a long, unfocused one.

210

Resist the urge to give your cellphone number and e-mail address to all and sundry. If you're serious about conserving your time for *you*, treat these details as you treat your bank account.

(And fear not. The important messages will reach you.
They always do.)

211

Communication is the bridge between where you are now and where you want to be.

Without communication, nothing changes.

Communication is everyone's responsibility.
But communication *management* needs an owner.

(What would happen if Finance or Production had no owner?)

Distracting sidebars and irrelevant sub-plots
suck the energy from letters, documents and speeches
with the efficiency of a bilge pump.

Decide what your point is, and make it.
Everything else should support your case.
If it doesn't, then dump it.

214

Testing One. Testing One-TWO. One-TWO. One. One. One-TWO, One-two-three. Testing One. One. Puh-Puh-Puh. Sssssss. Sssss. Testing. Testing. One-TWO.....

PLEASE. Check out the PA system *befcre* the audience arrives!

That's just the way it is, we say.

But the way things are is the direct result of how we respond
and adjust to events. Events *we* create, responses *we* choose.

No matter how much you might wish it otherwise, everything you
do and say, and everything you stand for, contributes
to your moment by moment reality. *The way things are*.

You're always broadcasting.

216

When you're in conversation with someone,
have the courtesy to turn off your cellphone
or divert your calls.

If you really can't,
say that you're likely to be interrupted, and why.

217

When was the last time you asked yourself:

What impression am I giving?
What impression does my company make?

Perhaps today's the day?

218

The more technology we use,
the more the world needs face-to-face contact.

219

Know what your principles and values are, and stick to them.

They won't always be the ones that prevail, but people will know where you stand, and respect you for your steadfastness.

(Besides, blowing like a flag in the wind
wastes energy and disturbs your sleep.)

220

Managers who want to communicate
often mistake the means for the end.

But communication wins through
on the strength of the architecture first,
not the bricks and mortar.

The strategy, not the technique.

221

Again and again, surveys show communication to be the core skill that separates leaders from managers.

And ahead of talent or technique comes *attitude* to communication: believing in it, knowing it's important, and *wanting* to communicate.

Communication *is* management at work.

222

Shy or self-conscious behaviour is rooted in 'me' focus.

Care less about the impression you're making and more about the other person, and your shyness will melt away.

(Are you really *that* fascinating?)

Employees need to feel their work is meaningful in the context of the bigger picture. There needs to be a clear line of sight between their input and the company's output.

And that's a job only communication can do.

Four stages of knowing

DATA
Raw material. Facts and figures in their basic state.

INFORMATION
Data in a form that can be accessed and used.

KNOWLEDGE
Information interpreted by brainpower and experience.

WISDOM
Knowledge tempered by reflection.

225

It's easy to acquire information or knowledge.

But it's only through *reflection*, when we have an opportunity to access our intuition — so easily buried in the din of daily activity — that we can make the journey from knowledge to wisdom.

And, more than information or knowledge,
in every aspect of our lives today,
we need wisdom.

226

Bad language rarely illuminates.

In the Dark Ages, communication was about
'keeping the troops happy'. Missiles fired from above told
the troops what someone upstairs thought they should know.

Today we have to move faster. Be flexible. Ready to respond.
On our toes. *In touch*. And communication is the energy.
The *means*.

Only by keeping your finger on the pulse of the organisation,
can you be in touch. And only by being in touch,
can you be in the race.

Strategic and creative skill — the vital *thinking* part — should precede all communication exercises.

If you don't have it on board, hire it in.

229

The higher up the totem pole, the thicker the fog.
And in the fog and fudge of corporate politicking
the truth is harder to find, and harder to speak.

The communication challenge — especially at the top — is to be
open to the truth, and have the courage to speak it.

If we can't speak the truth, we can't be ourselves.
And if we can't be ourselves, work can become
hollow and without meaning.

230

Eye-contact is critical when speaking to a group.
It's easy for some people to feel excluded
if your gaze is anchored to one spot.

Like the hands on a clock, shift your attention regularly
from one time-check to another.

231

If you must criticise, criticise the behaviour, not the person.
And never consciously hurt someone's feelings
or make them feel inferior.

No matter how much the behaviour deserves to be condemned, the *person* deserves to be respected.

232

Communication is: a builder of 'community'.

233

It's easy to stick to the point in a normal exchange.
But in a quarrel, when emotion takes over and sparks fly
in all directions, we can easily lose our way.

When this happens, remember that the past is gone and the future
hasn't arrived yet, and *concentrate* on the present moment.

(Any sailor can keep a ship on course in calm seas.
It takes a skilled seaman to stay on course in a storm!)

The truth is always simple.

Avoiding it, putting it off, pretending things are different or otherwise muddying the water, are all very successful ways of making communication complex.

If people are prepared to contribute some of their time on this planet to hearing you speak, have the courtesy to

- Be prepared
- Be informed
- Be focused
- Be clear
- Be truthful
- Be *interesting*!

236

Remember: the on/off switch is in the audience's hand.
Not yours.

237

*H*earing and *listening* are not the same.

Hearing happens in the ear.
Listening happens in the heart.

238

What have we decided? *Who* needs to know? *What* do we say? *How* do we say it? *When* do we say it? And *who's* responsible?

Help communication become a good habit.
Stitch it into every agenda.

239

Trust cannot be given, created, cultivated, generated, granted, developed — or bought.

Trust can only be earned.

240

Listening is an art that improves with practice.

Tuned-in to your own internal monologue means tuned-out to the world. Rediscover the rich tapestry of sound around you:

Wind in the leaves. Water gurgling and gushing.
Birdsong. Footsteps. The murmur of voices.

The symphony of Life.

241

Change of the human kind
happens *only* through communication.

Communication is the *driver* of change.

242

Managers readily accept communication as an important success factor. Even critical. Yet for many, it remains an untested theory.

Those who make the transition from theory to practice discover the simple truth: You can manage communication. Or be managed *by* it. That's the choice.

Those who don't are most vulnerable in the increasingly complex world of business.

243

Always try to see the good in people.

Most people are good people. The good ones are good people having a good day. The others are good people having a bad day.

244

Group synergy isn't automatic. It's the product of *the way* people in the group interact with each other.

It happens when personal 'baggage' is set aside and different points of view are treasured, not trampled. It's there when members of the group are inspired by one another. When we feel: 'We're on a roll' or 'We just jelled'.

In synergy the combined effect of the whole is greater than the sum of the individual parts. In other words, we achieve more *together* than we ever could individually.

(Synergy should be the aim of all groups.)

245

If something is complex, find a way to simplify it. Making it easy to understand doesn't make it trivial.

246

We connect brain-to-brain, not mouth-to-mouth.

247

Every time you communicate with someone,
you're just one of many alternatives, distractions,
and loyalties competing for attention.

The communication challenge is to maximise
the possibility of being heard and understood.

248

We trust some of our senses more than others.

Some people are most alert to *visual* information.
Others prefer information gathered *auditorily*.
And *kinaesthetic* people are more sensitive to touch and feelings.

When you know your own preference you'll understand
how people can suddenly shut down when approached
in the 'wrong' language.

249

Visually-sensitive people use visual expressions:
'I *see* it clearly', 'How does it *look*?', 'What's the big *picture*', '*Show me* what you mean'.

Use analogies and word-pictures to connect with your 'visual' friends, and talk about how things *look*. Support your argument with images and diagrams. And for choice, avoid the phone.

250

Auditorily-sensitive people use sound words: 'I *hear* what you say', 'That *sounds* good', 'We're *on the same wavelength*', '*Spell it out* for me'.

Engage your 'auditorial' friends by varying the tone and pace of your conversation. Describe how things *sound*, and choose words that are pleasant or interesting to listen to. The phone's good.

251

Kinaesthetically-sensitive people use 'feeling' words: '*Hold on* a minute', 'I *sense* from you', 'Do you have *hands-on* experience?', 'Can you put me *in touch with*..?'

Your 'kinaesthetic' friends will appreciate tactile words to describe things — rough as sandpaper, smooth as glass — and expressions that tell them how people *feel*. And whenever possible, speak with them in person.

When you reach a communication cul-de-sac,
∙∙∙∙∙∙check your assumptions:

Are you starting in the right place?
Are you focused on the symptom or the cause?
Are you looking for a simple answer to a complex problem?

Are you trying to solve the *right* problem?

253

Become known as a person who keeps promises and meets commitments. Communicate 'dependability'.

254

Values don't exist 'out there' someplace.
They're communicated in everything
the organisation says and does.

Among the happiest places to work are places
where the organisation's values and
the personal values of its people are in sync.

255

People can't read and listen at the same time.

If you really feel the urge to use slides with words, have the savvy to quit talking and give the audience a chance to read, before continuing.

(Slides with very few words are best.
Slides with pictures and *no* words are even better.)

256

Don't accept woolly thinking. Insist on clarity.
In the long run, clarity saves time and avoids heartache.

Avoid the pitfalls of second-rate listening
  (*Difficult yes, but really important*):

- Leave your personal baggage outside. *Don't prejudge.*
- Say Ssshhh to your self-talk. Don't rehearse your response.
- Be open to the message. *Even unpleasant ones.*
- Listen beyond style. Good or bad, don't let performance impede your listening.

Organisations don't change. *People* change.

Know your audience. One-to-one or one-to-many, when the message doesn't relate to the audience, the audience won't relate to the message.

(No matter how prepared you are, if your assumptions about your audience and *their* objectives are off course, you're destined to miss the mark.)

260

Sooner or later every business issue
becomes a communication issue.

261

'I have a dream...'
'Ask not what your country can do for you...'
'All for one and one for all...'
'My life is my message...'

Never underestimate the power — and the *staying power* — of a simple message.

262

Mismatched expectations
are the source of much interpersonal grief.

So when you ask someone to do something,
make it absolutely clear what you expect
in terms of what, and how, and when.

And *check* for understanding.

Don't claim to be open with your employees
if there's anything you're not prepared to share.

In a high-trust environment, there are no secrets.

264

Why put a desk between you and the other person?

Step out from your comfort zone. Sit on the same side. It's much more friendly, and friendly meetings are more productive.

265

Dirty or out-of-date slides carry their own message.

266

Good Communication Housekeeping Tip:

Periodically ask yourself:
Is what I'm saying or doing
adding to the confusion?

267

When a lot depends on a particular letter or presentation, shifting your focus from *What do I want to say?* to *What do I want to happen?* will help you choose the best words and phrases.

268

Communication never stops.

You can mis-communicate, you can under-communicate and you can over-communicate. But you can't *not* communicate.

You may think and behave as if you are separate from others.
But you are not.

Apart from our fundamental human need to socialise,
interacting with others is necessary to get things done.
A super-interdependency permeates all aspects of our lives.

It's only when we step out from the trenches of our daily
endeavour and leave our personal attachments aside,
that we become sensitive to our connectedness.

From a distance we can see the truth: There are no boundaries.

270

We work in an inside-out way.

Just as you are what you eat, you are what you think.
Out of your mind comes your response to everything around you.
Every response is governed by what you think.

'I think, therefore I am.'

271

The person who answers the telephone represents the organisation and *everything* it stands for. In that moment they *are* the organisation.

Every time the phone rings is an opportunity to score a goal. Or drop the ball.

Consider yourself equal. And treat others equally.

'Rank' is a just way of being organised — not a statement of value. Don't let it get in the way.

In truth, there is no 'above'. And no 'below'.

273

Using *'we'* and *'us'* instead of *'I'* helps to build co-operation between you and the other person. Always talking about what *'I want...'* or *'I think...'* or *'I feel...'* makes it clear where *your* priorities lie.

Good communication addresses the needs of *both* parties.

274

Beware of the tendency to 'punish' people you disagree with or dislike by just *pretending* to listen.

275

If it took you three years to discover where your organisation should be going, how can you expect your people to grasp it in three hours?

Understanding takes time and patience.

276

Meetings are not platforms for airing pet loves and hates, so leave your hobby-horse safely tethered *outside* the door.

Walls serve to keep things out as well as keep things in, and they can easily block the view.

When you find it hard to see the other point of view, could it be the walls you've built around your views are getting in the way?

278

Genuine dialogue requires you
to be in touch with all of your emotions.

In most things it's important to start well.
With communication, it's critical.

Writing a letter, making a speech or meeting someone for the first time, recovering from a bad start is always an uphill climb.

280

Good communication is the No.1 ingredient in lasting relationships of every kind.

Business is dominated by logic and references to what we *think*. But humans are *feeling* beings, and feelings are always present.

When you sense that communication is drying up because of trapped emotion, take the risk of meeting feelings head-on. Ask what people *feel*. And challenge answers that begin 'Well, I *think*....'

Feelings and needs are always at the heart of the matter.

282

The human goal must be to make each moment
the best that it can be. For all concerned.

No interaction is unimportant.
Even small moments with strangers,
that may seem insignificant at the time,
are important pieces of Life's jigsaw.

Yours — and theirs.

283

The human mind is uncomfortable with information gaps so it joins the dots and completes our picture of 'reality' — based on assumptions.

Assumptions, especially about people, can lead to heartache. So don't assume it. Confirm it.

284

Don't be afraid to reveal your inner self.

Appropriate self-disclosure is the hallmark of authentic conversation.

285

If you did a communication check on your important relationships right now, would you answer 'Yes' or 'No' to:

I can talk openly about the things that concern me.
I listen enough. And I feel listened to.
I invest enough time in just *being* with those who matter.

And what would *they* say?

286

When communication reaches stalemate, ask:

What can the other person *see* that I can't see?
What do they *feel* that I don't feel?

Communication is one of the last frontiers where significant improvement can be leveraged in the workplace.

It's the key that unlocks continuous improvement.

288

Within the walls of an organisation, it's easy to abdicate personal responsibility. You can come to believe you are not representing yourself. That you're just part of the 'system'. Carrying out orders. And you can *even* believe you have no choice.

But *when* do you have *no* choice? There's always a line between right and wrong. It's always there, somewhere. Can you allow someone else to decide for you, where it should lie?

Listening is harder work than talking. Good listening means:

- Listening actively
- Listening critically
- Listening for the complete meaning
- Listening with empathy
- Listening with an open mind

290

Interpersonal friction is often an attempt by someone
to gain control and establish 'certainty'.

Come to terms with two unassailable facts:
You are not in control (even when you think you are).
And at its most certain, life is ambiguous.

Now will you relax?

Communication is a core management competence.

(Unfortunately, communication is often
a core management *in*competence.)

Aware of it or not, every group grapples with two main issues: Purpose and Process.

Purpose is the group's raison d'etre.
The answer to: *Why* are we here?

Process is the way things get done.
The answer to: *How* do we behave together?

Don't let Purpose rule the day. Only by fully attending to *both* will you open the door to group synergy.

293

Don't expect people to concentrate or communicate effectively when they're emotionally hijacked.

294

Last line first.

If you're finding it hard to start a letter, think about how you will end it. Sometimes what you write as a summary in closing, can be a good way to begin.

295

Compromise is about being *genuinely* willing to modify or change your view, however cherished it may be.

Effective, two-way communication is crucial to the growth and maintenance of the strong relationships that can contribute so much to the ultimate success of an organisation.

If that doesn't exist, it must be built.
Step-by-step, consistently and over time.

Openness. Honesty. Truth. Respect. Authenticity.

These words appear frequently throughout this book because
they are the golden keys to effective communication.
If any one of them is missing, the interaction is diminished.

Self-awareness is the first step on the road to better communication. Make a start by raising to conscious thought some of the unconscious processes that drive your attitudes and behaviour.

What is it that makes you what you are?

299

Formulas sound attractive, but there are no formulas for communication. If there were, everyone would be using them. What works on one occasion may nose-dive on the next.

> There's nothing for it but to respond
> to the real need of the moment.

300

Never let the sun go down on your anger, goes the old saying.
And it's good advice.

Relationship difficulties that drag into another day
are harder to resolve. So sort it out today if you can.

301

Communication isn't easy.

If it was, there'd be no conflict.
And the whole human race would be
One Big Happy Family.

But when you pick it up and shake it around
and see how it works, a light goes on
and you begin to understand what you've got your hands on.

Something very big.

The power to transform your world — one relationship at a time.

We're always looking for better ways of working and being together. And the wisdom is everywhere. If you'd like to share a personal communication tip that works for you, we'd love to hear from you at the address below. If your thought appears in future books, your contribution will be acknowledged.

downey youell associates
123 Lower Baggot Street
Dublin 2
Ireland

INDEX

action, 169, 185, 188
anger, 66, 300
apologising, 117
appearance, 184
assumptions, 129, 130, 184, 186, 252, 259, 283
attending, 176, 204, 282
attitudes, 30, 92, 161, 221, 272
audience, 29, 48, 53, 87, 93, 168, 200, 230, 236

authenticity, 95, 114, 284, 295, 297
avoidance, 14, 101, 122, 135, 234, 281, 300
awareness, 74, 138, 215, 301,

bad news, 205
barriers, 66, 73, 81, 101, 129, 277, 293
brain, 15, 70, 193, 246, 283

certainty, 25, 145, 277, 290

change, 128, 156, 174, 211, 241, 258, 270
clarity, 24, 42, 58, 132, 182, 256, 262, 266
co-operation, 27, 58, 81, 180, 273
compassion, 32, 79, 86
competence, 137, 203, 291
confidence, 107, 206, 222
conflict, 14, 59, 79, 92, 122, 135, 203, 290
connectedness, 1, 102, 269
content, 11, 26, 41, 53, 103, 153, 173, 202, 267
context, 151, 200
conversation, 51, 55, 112, 164, 284, 266
courtesy, 65, 72, 89, 187, 216

credibility, 8, 40, 60, 67, 71, 150
criticism, 183, 231
culture, 5, 45, 110, 155

data, 49, 224, 225
decisiveness, 172
definition, 1, 5, 11, 13, 33, 97, 123, 154, 211, 232, 268, 301
dialogue, 278
disagreement, 14, 25, 59, 79, 148, 233
disclosure, 20, 146, 284
dishonesty, 19, 119
distrust, 2, 101
diversity, 18, 159
documents, 91, 136, 144, 213

dominance, 73, 96, 198
dress, 73

e-mail, 77, 109, 175, 210
emotion, 66, 108, 233, 278, 281, 293
empathy, 54, 79, 90, 286
employees, 102, 110, 126, 156, 177, 188, 195, 223, 227, 271
enthusiasm, 76
equality, 40, 272
ethics, 288
evaluation, 38, 149

face-to-face, 44, 175, 218
fairness, 189
feedback, 106, 188

focus, 12, 41, 213, 233, 267
formulas, 201, 299

gender, 99
getting attention, 23, 87, 247
groups, 4, 14, 70, 106, 120, 124, 244, 292

hidden agendas, 101

image, 118, 170, 195, 217, 265, 271
impact, 100, 116, 140, 157, 178, 193, 247, 261, 267
impression, 62, 136, 147, 170, 217, 265, 279
information, 17, 224, 225

information overload, 21, 77, 109, 210
inner voice, 98, 204, 240
intuition, 31, 225

jargon, 124
judgement, 9, 83
junk mail, 21, 109

knowledge, 224, 225

language, 36, 84, 124, 191, 226, 273
leaders, 4, 113, 120, 155, 177, 221

letters, 21, 36, 65, 125, 147, 157, 209, 213, 267, 279, 294
listening, 3, 28, 43, 78, 98, 139, 162, 176, 237, 240, 257, 274, 285, 289

management, 212, 229, 242, 291
meaning, 11, 17, 24, 49, 97, 151
meetings, 28, 34, 120, 158, 207, 238, 264, 276
mental maps, 18, 25, 94
messages, 41, 97, 140
metaphors, 22, 116

names, 55, 125
non-verbal, 37, 44, 47, 57, 62, 75, 76, 83, 96, 115, 134, 152, 165, 179, 184, 185, 190, 198, 230

observation, 9, 31, 204
open mind, 2, 20, 104, 167, 174, 199, 295
openness, 180, 263, 285, 297
organisations, 5, 38, 40, 45, 67, 80, 102, 110, 118, 142, 149, 151, 154, 155, 156, 160, 169, 177, 180, 186, 191, 201, 212, 217, 220, 221, 227, 229, 258, 260, 263, 271, 287, 296

pace, 196
perception, 25, 82, 94, 199
personal space, 46
personality, 159
persuasion, 64, 128, 192
physiognomy, 179
praise, 105
preparation, 12, 38, 60, 150, 163, 186
presentation, 7, 16, 23, 60, 87, 93, 131, 150, 153, 157, 168, 200, 214, 235, 236, 255, 259, 279
presenter, 29, 35, 48, 71, 133, 196, 230
principles, 219

process, 11, 292
purpose, 158, 189, 223, 292

reality, 1, 82, 199, 215
reflection, 224, 225
relationships, 6, 10, 32, 122, 190, 194, 243, 280, 285, 301
relevance, 53, 109, 126, 259
reputation, 9, 170, 195, 253, 271
respect, 34, 39, 46, 63, 72, 231, 243, 282, 297
responsibility, 10, 50, 88, 92, 109, 212, 288

self knowledge, 54, 111, 129, 208, 270, 285, 298

senses, 248, 249, 250, 251
service, 39, 63
shyness, 222
silence, 75
simplifying, 245 261
slides, 16, 60, 150, 182, 255, 265
slogans, 80, 178
speeches, 16, 153, 261
stalemate, 252, 286
starting, 279, 294
stereotyping, 121
stories, 22
strategy, 160, 163, 169, 220, 228
synchronicity, 40, 134, 195, 254
synergy, 244

talking, 78, 143, 169
technology, 33, 35, 60, 61, 77, 166, 175, 214, 218
telephone, 12, 44, 72, 77, 85, 89, 127, 181, 187, 210, 216, 271
thinking, 31, 130, 163, 174, 228, 256, 270
tone, 71, 85
trust, 2, 39, 52, 180, 239, 263
truth, 19, 104, 114, 197, 205, 229, 234, 297
two-way, 176, 227, 296

understanding, 13, 42, 59, 141, 262, 275

values, 30, 40, 142, 155, 219, 254
vision, 156, 171, 177
voice, 71, 85, 115
voicemail, 89, 175

wisdom, 69, 202, 224, 225
withholding, 20, 104, 146
words, 30, 56, 68, 84, 100, 112, 161, 178, 185, 273
writing, 26, 91, 157, 209, 213, 294